Original title:
Navigating Life Without a Compass


Copyright © 2025 Creative Arts Management OÜ
All rights reserved.


Author: Liam Sterling
ISBN HARDBACK: 978-1-80566-015-6
ISBN PAPERBACK: 978-1-80566-310-2

## Rebalancing in the Storm

My ship's shape is quite absurd,
Sailing straight, so often slurred.
The map is upside down, oh dear,
I guess I'll just drink my beer.

With waves that dance like rabbits do,
A seagull squawks, 'Hey, how are you?'
I wave back, it's quite the show,
Who needs a course? Let's go with flow!

The stars are lost, the sun is shy,
My crew is made of cheese and pie.
"Ahoy!" I shout, "Let's make a toast!"
To sailing straight—well, that's a boast!

The wind's a prankster, pulling slack,
With laughter loud, no room for lack.
A lighthouse flickers, dim and lame,
But sailing's fun, it's all a game!

## Guiding Light in the Abyss

In dark of night, I lost my way,
My map just laughed, 'Go out and play!'
I tripped on dreams, sat on a rock,
While owls hooted, I tried to talk.

My GPS gave a cheeky wink,
Said, "Free yourself, just stop and think!"
I waved goodbye to all my fears,
And danced with shadows, drank some beers.

## Unfolding Mysteries of the Open Road

With eyes closed tight, I hit the gas,
The road unwound, I felt a blast!
A sign said 'left,' so I went right,
Ended up at a llama's sight.

The world is odd, I spun around,
Found a circus truck, lost and found.
I juggled snacks, my heart so bold,
In this strange life, I struck gold.

## Rafts of Dreams on an Endless Sea

I sailed on thoughts, a raft so fine,
With rubber ducks and cheap red wine.
The waves just giggled, splashed my face,
In this odd boat, I found my place.

The horizon teased, it waved hello,
I flipped my sail where the wild winds blow.
Mermaids winked and sang a tune,
Underneath a grinning moon.

## The Edge Between the Known and Unknown

I'm on a cliff with squirrels galore,
Their nutty chatter I can't ignore.
They point me to the edge of fate,
Where life's a joke and we all skate.

The path I tread may twist and bend,
With silly signs that pretend to mend.
But laughter lights the darkest trail,
In this wild life, I shall not fail.

## Lost Among the Stars

I aimed for Mars, hit a tree,
Why is space full of debris?
My rocket's just a tin can,
With a steering wheel from a van.

I ask a squirrel for some tips,
He just nods, takes a few sips.
The stars are bright, but oh so far,
Should've brought snacks while raising the bar.

## The Uncharted Path Ahead

I took a trail less explored,
Found a frog who played the lord.
He said, 'Go left, or was it right?'
I'll follow him, he's quite a sight.

My map's a doodle on a napkin,
With arrows pointing, but I'm trapped in.
Turns out the path's a bumpy ride,
With more twists than a carnival slide.

## Wandering Souls in a Mapless World

We roam with flair, without a clue,
GPS? Nah, we'll wing it too!
The sun sets low, we still lose track,
It's a game where no one gets back.

We'll dance with paths that bob and weave,
And laugh at maps we can't believe.
With stars as guides, we're lost but free,
Two wandering souls and a cup of tea.

## The Driftwood's Journey

A piece of wood on an endless spree,
Riding waves, oh so carefree.
The ocean laughs as I float past,
With barnacles as my crew at last.

No compass to steer my little ride,
Just a seagull who squawks with pride.
I don't know where I'll end my quest,
But hey, driftwood's life is simply the best!

## **Paths Made of Questions**

Why is the sky so blue and bright?
Is it a reflection of my plight?
Am I walking in circles or just a square?
Every twist and turn leads to nowhere.

Where do the lost socks go at night?
Do they dance and sing in pure delight?
My map is a riddle, a game of chance,
I'll just follow the ducks in their dance.

If I ask the trees for some advice,
Will they whisper secrets or just think twice?
I might just trip over my own two feet,
Or discover a world that's kind of sweet.

## Beyond the Familiar Horizon

I peeked beyond the fence so stout,
Found a place I can't figure out.
Invisible lines I've never crossed,
My sanity here might just be lost.

The neighbors are aliens, it's plain to see,
With antennas bobbing like trees by the sea.
They barter in giggles and trade in snacks,
I'll join their crew, no need to relax.

I climbed a hill to watch the stars,
But all I found were candy bars.
I'll map my route with chocolate trails,
And sail on dreams with fluffy gales.

## Sailing on Unfamiliar Seas

The ship's a snack bar made of bread,
With sodas that bubble above your head.
Our compass spins like a confused cat,
While sailboats rust in the alley flat.

The fish wear hats and throw a dance,
Underwater jigs that will make you prance.
I'm lost at sea with a spoon as my oar,
Rowing to places I've never been before.

The sun's a pizza, melting away,
We navigate this lunch hour's play.
With jellybean sextants and gumdrop waves,
We're sailors of luck on sugar-brave graves.

## The Silence of Direction

In a world where maps like whispers creep,
I take my chances, and then I leap.
The signs are shy, they look away,
As I mumble my thoughts, day by day.

Directions are puzzles, my mind's not keen,
I found a banana, it looked like a screen.
I followed a cat that led me astray,
When all I wanted was just to play.

So here I stand with no clue in sight,
Dancing with shadows when it feels right.
I'll spin in circles, it's quite a dance,
In this silent game, I'll take my chance.

## Guiding Lights in the Dark

When shadows loom and paths grow dim,
I tiptoe forward, oh so grim.
A flashlight's dead, my phone's on mute,
Perhaps a raccoon's got the loot!

With every step, I hear a thud,
Is that a friend or just some mud?
I laugh, I trip, I lose the way,
But hey, it's just another day!

## **The Compass of the Heart**

They say to follow what you feel,
But sometimes love's a spinning wheel.
A tug to left, a pull to right,
Is it the heart or just a bite?

With chocolate dreams and coffee spills,
I chase a whim, I chase the thrills.
The heart's a map at best, I guess,
But sometimes ends up in a mess!

## When Signs Are Lost

I missed that turn, I cursed the fate,
A sign that said to simply wait.
Instead, I ended up in town,
Where laughter's loud and lifts the frown.

I thought I'd end at destination fun,
But here I am, all out of run.
With ice cream cones and silly hats,
Who knew the wrong way led to that?

## **Heartbeats Under Starlight**

Beneath the stars, I lost my shoe,
The night seems blurry, is that you?
With every giggle, I lose my grip,
But hey, this dance is quite a trip!

The cosmos twinkle, I sway and twirl,
The universe shouts, "Give it a whirl!"
With heartbeats bouncing to moonlit tunes,
I'm lost in laughter, beneath the moons!

## In Search of Wayfarers

I set out with my shoes untied,
My map was blank, my sights were wide.
I waved to squirrels, asked for the way,
They scampered off, not keen to stay.

A path of breadcrumbs led me astray,
I tripped on roots while some ducks would play.
A sign post spun, 'Turn left or right?',
I chose a bush and daydreamed of flight.

## The Dance of the Wayward Traveler

In a town where time forgot the clock,
I disco danced with a playful rock.
The pigeons roosted, judgmental, loud,
As I twisted and spun, feeling quite proud.

With every stumble and misshaped twirl,
I caught the eye of a frumpy girl.
We laughed as we fell, the world was a blur,
In chaotic rhythm, we danced with a purr.

## Compasses of the Soul

I asked my heart where to go today,
It shrugged and hummed, 'Just find a café.'
So off I wandered, mug in hand,
With sticky notes, my own life planned.

The latte art was a compass rose,
With cinnamon swirls, all eyes on my nose.
I journeyed through taste, each sip a delight,
But forgot my car keys - oh what a sight!

## Unseen Banners of Purpose

I marched with banners, invisible thread,
Each one whispered, 'Not sure, go ahead!'
A parade of thoughts, all wild and free,
Led me to stumble on a bumblebee.

I wore mismatched socks, my crown of dreams,
Waving at passing clouds, bursting at the seams.
With laughter my guide and goofiness my tune,
I found my path beneath a dancing moon.

## The Threads of Serendipity

Woke up this morning, no clue where to go,
A map in my pocket, but it's missing the show.
I stumbled on tacos, that filled me with glee,
Spun around in circles, then fell into a tree.

The sun set on paths that I dared not to trace,
I tripped on a sidewalk, but laughed at the pace.
A squirrel waved at me, perhaps he could steer,
I just followed laughter, for that was quite clear.

So here's to the roads that twist and they bend,
In the chaos of travel, I found a good friend.
No compass to guide me, just smiles and some pie,
Life's a wild adventure, now pass me the pie!

## Fractured Routes

I had a fine plan, it was genius, they said,
But lost in a maze, I followed my head.
Found a signpost smirking, with directions askew,
But hey, what's an error if laughed into view?

I turned left for coffee, then right for a snack,
And somehow, I wound up beneath a great stack.
Of pancakes and syrup, and oh what a sight,
I must be quite skilled at missing the flight!

With each step I take, I find treasures anew,
Like a donut shop's window, with sprinkles for two.
Though my route seems a puzzle, it's filled with delight,
Who needs a straight path when you can just bite?

## A Heart Without Coordinates

My heart feels like mercury, bouncing around,
Attraction's my compass but oh, I've been drowned.
In love's wild jungle, I swing from a vine,
Sipping hot cocoa, with a dash of sunshine.

Fresh starts in the fall, new leaps in the spring,
I search for affection, but what's it to bring?
The laugh of a stranger, a wink from a friend,
Who knew that lost journeys could twist and they bend?

I tumble through flirting, and smile off the beat,
With no maps in my pocket, I still find my seat.
What's lost may be funny, a dance in the dark,
For life can be better without leaving a mark.

## **Silent Streets and Open Skies**

In quiet little corners where silence does dwell,
I wander through laughter, just shedding my shell.
Each street holds a secret, I dive into fun,
Like finding old socks, or shoes lost from one.

The stars twinkle softly, like winks from the past,
I trip on my thoughts, oh my, what a blast!
With open skies cheering and no clue in sight,
I turn wrong into right, and keep up the fight.

So here's to exploring with glee on my face,
Through silent old streets, I find my own pace.
Without maps, I'm grateful, for joy is the prize,
In this wild, wacky world, beneath unlimited skies.

## Signals from the Unknown

When life's a game of charades,
And you're lost in the masquerade,
The GPS says, 'You have arrived!'
But the nearest place is where you thrived.

A squirrel's your guide on this wild quest,
With acorns and nuts; it knows the rest.
But as you follow, with laughter and cheer,
You realize it's leading you to nowhere near.

A signpost twirls; what's that all about?
Is that a 'yes' or a 'no' in doubt?
With every turn, you wipe your eyes,
Is that a mirage or truth in disguise?

You wave at clouds for a sign or two,
They giggle back, then rain on you.
Just let loose, follow your heart's own sound,
For life's a stage, where the lost are found.

## Threads of Instinct

With threads of gut, we weave our way,
Through alleyways bright and clouds of gray.
A cat knows better, with its sly little twist,
Yet we trip over shoelaces, can't resist.

A fork in the trail that decides our fate,
One path leads to joy, the other's just late.
You take a chance, toss a coin in the air,
Heads or tails—do I even care?

Around the corner, there's a dance of fate,
A chicken in the road—you've sealed your fate!
So you sidestep it, with a laugh and a jump,
Realizing the world's just one big clump.

Trust your instincts, they're always a hoot,
Like wearing mismatched shoes, oh what a route!
Life's a thread, frayed and spun tight,
Let go and twirl, you might just take flight.

## Directions in the Dark

With a flashlight that's dead and a glow of dread,
You wander like zombies, just follow the spread.
Which way's up, and where's the down?
In this topsy-turvy, head-spinning town.

You ask a raccoon for help, it just sneers,
And rolls its eyes, confirming your fears.
Each turn's a giggle, a bump in the night,
As you trip over roots in this bumbled fright.

A map is crumpled, but hey, it's an art,
Your sense of direction's a real work of heart.
Stand in a circle, spin around thrice,
Now you're confused, but oh, isn't it nice?

In the dark, there's joy—just feel the thrill,
Every wrong turn can lead you to chill.
So dance with shadows, don't make a fuss,
In the chaos, my friend, you'll find your plus.

## Footprints in the Sand of Uncertainty

Footprints in the sand tell tales of the lost,
Each step a riddle, no matter the cost.
You run from the waves, but they're hotter still,
Chasing your dreams just adds to the thrill.

With flip-flops on wrong, you're off to the chase,
You're navigating life like a chicken in lace.
Bumbling and tripping, you laugh at the breeze,
Each grain a reminder—just aim to please.

The sun sets low; the shadows grow long,
You start to dance as if you belong.
With every misstep, your laughter is loud,
Brighter than stars in a sky of a crowd.

So follow those footprints, wild and free,
In the sand of uncertainty, just let it be.
For every wrong turn is a step for delight,
And life's one big joke—so hold on tight!

## **The Pathless Journey**

With no map in hand, I roam,
Bumping into trees like it's home.
Every turn a new surprise,
A squirrel stares with judgmental eyes.

Stumbling over roots and stones,
Doing the dance of clumsy clones.
Each mishap a tale spun bright,
Laughter echoes through the night.

A compass? Nah, I'm too cool,
Follow the ducks, and that's my rule.
They quack along the water's edge,
While I step back from the ledge.

Yet every twist leads me to cheer,
Found a field of daisies near.
Life's a puzzle, quirky and fun,
No navigation—just run, baby, run!

## **Drifting Through Shadows**

In twilight's glow, shadows play,
I wander lost, yet here I stay.
With giggles caught in every breeze,
Life's a puzzle made with ease.

A blindfold on, I spin around,
Chasing laughter, never found.
I trip on clouds, I slip on light,
A dance of chaos, pure delight.

Where am I headed? Who can tell?
Onward to the funniest hell.
With every wrong turn, I grin wide,
Life's a rollercoaster ride!

So here I am, no plan at hand,
Just tickling giggles, grains of sand.
In the mist, I sway and sway,
Drifting through shadows, come what may!

## Echoes of Uncertainty

Every step's a question mark,
Lost in a field, I stumble, stark.
"Is that a path or just my feet?"
With laughter, life's a quirky treat.

Frogs leap by and croak in tune,
"Follow us, the right path's strewn!"
But they hop off with sly delight,
Leaving me puzzled in the night.

With echoes ringing in my ear,
I grasp at chances, drinks, and cheer.
Uncertainty's a charming friend,
With silly tales that never end.

So here I stand, a painted clown,
With painted smile, I won't back down.
In this wild dance of twists and bends,
I find the joy—the best of friends!

## The Art of Aimless Travel

With suitcase full of dreams to roam,
I wander off from what's called home.
No destination on my list,
Just whimsical paths, you get the gist.

Each coffee shop's a place to muse,
A spot to nap, to snooze and cruise.
With bated breath, I spot a cat,
I swear this life is where it's at!

Maps confused, my GPS is high,
I ask a pigeon, "What's nearby?"
He coos and fluffs, then flies away,
With newfound hope, I'll seize the day.

So here's to roads that twist and spin,
To right turns that may cause chagrin.
In aimless travel, we find our way,
Life's a circus—join the play!

## Among the Ruins of Certainty

In the land where plans all crumble,
A map's just a joke that makes you stumble.
I once had a guide, a wise old cat,
But he lost his sense under my old hat.

With every detour, laughter bubbles,
Each wrong turn ends in silly troubles.
I chose the path lined with rubber ducks,
But ended up knee-deep in muddy muck!

So here I stand, in my awkward stance,
Pretending to search for the next big chance.
The GPS whispers, "Just take a right,"
But my left foot goes, "No, let's take flight!"

Among these ruins, I take my pause,
Life's a circus, and I'm without laws.
I'll dance with the chaos, twirl with the breeze,
Who cares about roads? I'll just do as I please!

## Soliloquy of a Wayfarer

Oh, where does this road lead me, my friend?
I'd ask for directions, but where to begin?
The signpost is crooked, the trees start to chat,
And I can't seem to find my poor old hat.

I trip on my thoughts, and stumble on dreams,
Each step that I take, a new puzzle it seems.
With a laugh and a grin, I keep wandering free,
Like a lost little fish in a vast, open sea.

Should I follow the ants or that cloud up there?
They both look inviting, I've no time to spare.
With breadcrumbs I gather, I hope to remember,
That laughter and joy are my ways to endeavor.

So on I shall wander, with smile in my chest,
Through twists of confusion, I'll try to invest.
In a world full of chaos, I'll find my own fun,
As a wayfarer lost, but with warmth from the sun!

## The Perils of Footsteps Unmarked

I tiptoe through choices, the ground feels so slick,
In the land of the clueless, I'm lost, what a trick!
With footprints behind me that vanish like smoke,
I give a loud laugh, what a comical joke!

Once I took off on a wild rabbit chase,
But the rabbit turned out to be just my shoelace.
With shoes made of clouds, I dance on a whim,
In a jolly parade where the lights are so dim.

Each step is a gamble, with giggles in tow,
Should I leap for the moon or stick with the show?
The perils abound, but I can't seem to pout,
For every small fumble just makes me shout!

So let's toast to those who stray off the map,
With cupcakes and sparkles, no need for a nap.
Life's full of blunders, oh what a fine art,
In this dance of uncertainty, I'm just playing my part!

## Tides of Fate in Unknown Waters

In a boat built of laughter, I set sail with cheer,
With jellybean compasses, there's nothing to fear.
The tides of fate roll with a giggly embrace,
As I drift with the currents, there's joy in this space.

Shall I follow the waves or the wind in my hair?
With sea creatures chatting, who needs to prepare?
A dolphin named Larry shows me how to dive,
In the ocean of whimsy, I feel so alive!

The maps are for sailors who're serious and grim,
I'll write my own tale with a skip and a brim.
With treasure of giggles and gold made of cheer,
The unknown is bright, and there's nothing to fear.

So here's to the waters, mysterious and wild,
With each splash of adventure, I'm forever a child.
Tides of fate bring their own kind of fun,
In the dance of the sea, I'll twirl with the sun!

## The Rhythm of the Route

With socks of two shades, I dance my way,
The street signs laugh, leading me astray.
My shoes left footprints, quite out of sync,
I trip on my joy, it's fun, I think.

The map's upside down, but I'm not in a rush,
The pigeons coo loudly, they think I'm plush.
I order a latte at a burger stand,
Life's full of hiccups, oh isn't it grand?

I ask for directions, they point and chuckle,
Turns out the cafe's just behind the buckle.
I wave at a tree, it waves back too,
Every twist and turn brings something new.

So here's to the paths that twist and twine,
With each little turn, I sip my wine.
There's humor in chaos, in every misstep,
I'll waltz with the world, skip the prep.

## The Beauty of Unfamiliar Streets

The streetlights flicker, quite like my dance,
I wave at a cat who takes a strange stance.
A map in my pocket, but who needs that now?
Life's better with chaos, I'll take a bow.

I stumble on sidewalks, they make me their guest,
Each corner I turn, I'm put to the test.
A fountain is spouting, but not with water,
Instead, it's my laughter, oh what a daughter!

Some folks are staring, but I give a grin,
They're lost in their thoughts, I dive right in.
With ice cream drips staining my shirt and my hands,
I dance through the streets, ignoring the plans.

The beauty's in wandering, wonky and wide,
For every wrong turn, there's a joy to abide.
So let's toast to the roads that lead us astray,
In this funny old world, we'll find our way.

## Unraveled Paths

Like noodles untangled, my thoughts in a spin,
Each way that I wander breeds laughter within.
A coffee shop's sign points straight to my heart,
But I find a donut, so it's a fresh start.

A squirrel steals my sandwich, it gives me a wink,
I'll chase down my dreams, or at least, I'll think.
An umbrella's my shield when the rain drops laugh,
It juggles my snacks, oh what a gaff!

Lost in a maze where the GPS fails,
I create my own route with ships and with sails.
The statues are laughing, they know every trick,
I shimmy and giggle, this life's got a kick.

With each misfit moment, my joy reappears,
My compass is broken, but laughter's my gears.
So here's to the paths, all tangled and fun,
Unraveled adventures, we've only begun!

## The Colors of Aimless Journeys

With crayons of life, I color the road,
Each detour I take, my happiness flowed.
The sky's wearing polka dots, balloons in the trees,
At every new turn, I'm brought to my knees.

I found an old dinosaur stuck in a fence,
It smiled at me softly, made perfect sense.
A parade of my thoughts, with a float made of cheese,
Each nonsense adventure, such a quirky breeze.

The cookies are dancing, they're joining the show,
I trip on the frosting, oh where did it go?
With sprinkles of laughter, I wade through my bliss,
Each aimless excursion, a whimsical kiss.

In colors so bright, my heart skips a beat,
With no compass in hand, life's still oh so sweet.
So let's paint our days with a splash and a cheer,
In this rainbow of moments, I'll always steer.

## The Journey of the Blindfolded

I traipse through fields of daisies bright,
My shoes on the left, I swear they're right.
Left my map at home with the laundry list,
It's quite the adventure—too fun to resist!

I'll turn at the sound of a laughing goat,
Or follow the path of a wayward boat.
With each silly stumble, my spirits soar,
Who needs a compass when you can explore?

A squirrel gives directions, a crow quips too,
They say, 'Over there!'—I don't have a clue.
But laughter is guiding this fool on his quest,
Finding fortune in folly—life's little jest!

So here I march on, blindfolded with glee,
Each twist and each turn feels like comedy.
With my heart as my guide and no map in sight,
The journey is wild, and oh, what a fright!

## Unearthed Destinies

With my GPS broken, I meander alone,
Wearing mismatched socks that I found on the phone.
Each step is a riddle, each turn a surprise,
I trip over fate, and it's wearing disguise.

I peek in the bushes for treasures untold,
A sandwich, a shoe, pure vintage gold!
Bumping into strangers with socks as my map,
Who knew that confusion could lead to a clap?

A parade of lost socks floats by in the breeze,
Offering wisdom as I scrape off my knees.
"What's life without blunders?" the universe grins,
"Collect all your mishaps, and that's how it wins!"

So here's to the chaos, to paths that won't count,
To finding your fortune in every miscount.
The stars are my guide, and I dance with delight,
In the land of mayhem, I'm soaring in flight!

## Whispers of the Meandering Soul

I wander around like a lost little puppy,
With grass on my nose and my thoughts feeling muppy.
The road sings a tune that I can't quite recall,
I'm stepping on gum while I'm having a ball!

A caterpillar winks, says, 'You missed the train!'
I shrug and reply, 'But this sunshine's insane!'
With a hop and a skip, I dart sideways with flair,
Who needs direction when I dance in midair?

The squirrels are cheering, they throw acorns my way,
While a tortoise yells, "Dude, you've gone astray!"
But I grin and I twirl, laughter fills up the space,
In this wacky old world, I'm just keeping pace.

So here's to the journey, no ending in sight,
In a bubble of bliss, everything feels right.
With each whispered secret, embraced in the trees,
Life is a story best written with ease!

## Sanctuaries in the Wilderness

In the midst of the wild, my map's just a joke,
A raccoon points me left—oh, the things that he spoke!
I'm chasing my dreams, but they keep changing lanes,
Like a squirrel on espresso, oh, what a campaign!

The bushes are laughing as I stumble and bumble,
Finding my way through a jungle of tumble.
A creek sings a ballad, it teases my feet,
With each silly splash, life's a comedic feat!

I've built a fine fort from mismatched stones,
In the cozy of chaos, no worries or groans.
Whimsical thoughts float like leaves in the air,
Creating a haven wherever I dare.

So toast to the madness, the places I roam,
In the wilderness wide, I've found my true home.
With laughter my compass and joy as my guide,
Here's to life's wild ride with the world as my pride!

**The Stories We Carry**

We wander through the street, quite askew,
With tales that are strange in every hue.
In pockets, we stash dreams, both big and small,
Like misfit socks and marbles, we carry them all.

A map drawn in ketchup, a compass of cheese,
Life's questions like squirrels, they're sure to tease.
With laughter as our guide, we trip and we fall,
Each tumble a story we can't help but call.

Chasing after rainbows, we bop and we sway,
In flip-flops and sandals, we dance through the day.
Who needs a direction when the world is our play?
We spin like a top, come what may!

So join us on this ride, it's quite a sight,
With giggles and grins, we'll be alright.
Strange maps in our heads, hearts filled with glee,
In the circus of life, let's be wild and free!

## Hope in Empty Spaces

In rooms full of echoes, we shout with glee,
While shadows dance around, wild and free.
We fill up the voids with laughter so bright,
Creating new hopes in the stillness of night.

A cupboard of dreams, so dusty and bare,
We rummage through wishes found scattered everywhere.

With each empty corner, a smile appears,
Like finding old socks that remind us of years.

Our hearts are comedians, playing their part,
With jokes and with puns, they bring joy to the heart.
In spaces once barren, we plant funny seeds,
Watered by chuckles, they grow like wild weeds.

So here's to the gaps, let's dance in their light,
With laughter as compass, we'll be alright.
In the chaos we find hope, simple and true,
Filling empty spaces with giggles anew!

## Transitions in the Twilight

In the twilight we stumble, skinning our knees,
With stars as our friends, we take it with ease.
The sky gives us winks as the day begins to dim,
And shadows become allies in our goofy whim.

With flip-flops of wisdom and hats made of cheer,
We sidestep the troubles, we've nothing to fear.
The night wears a smile, it's willing to play,
As we fumble through moments, come what may.

Each stumble a step in a waltz that we share,
With twirls and with giggles, missteps in the air.
Transitions like popcorn, they pop in our brain,
Making laughter our partner in this silly game.

So hold onto the twilight, we'll dance till we drop,
Our hearts are the rhythm, let's never stop.
In each awkward moment, find joy, find delight,
As we glide through the dusk, together, so light!

## The Weight of Uncharted Waters

With a bucket for a boat, we sail through the blue,
In seas full of giggles, we'll chart something new.
Waves whisper secrets, like ducks with a plan,
As we float down the river with no masterful hand.

The fish wear a smile, they dance with great flair,
And seaweed's ticklish, it's quite a rare pair.
With jellyfish juggling and sandcastles tall,
We navigate waters that giggle and sprawl.

In puddles of chaos, we splash all about,
With rubber duck captains, we laugh and we shout.
The weight feels like feathers, the tide rolls just right,
As we sail on this sea of silliness tonight.

So here's to the waters, uncharted and free,
With hiccups and chuckles, come sail along with me.
For who needs a compass when laughter's the guide?
Let's float through the madness, adventures abide!

## Searching for North

I woke up one day, feeling quite lost,
Just me and my map, but I forgot the cost.
I pointed my finger, to find where to start,
   Turns out it's just a draw in the art.

The sun is glaring, and my drink is warm,
   Each step leads me far from the norm.
   I ask a bird, 'Are you north?' too,
It chirps back, 'Dude, I've got things to do!'

## Footprints in the Fog

In a world of clouds, where sights are unclear,
I trudge through the mist, mixing laughter with fear.
Each step I take, like dancing on air,
Toward shadows unknown, I'm light as a prayer.

I see someone's footprints, leading away,
Should I follow closely, or just play?
It's fun to pretend, I know where they lead,
But maybe it's just a raccoon with a bead!

## Whispers of the Wind

The wind said something, but I couldn't quite catch,
Was it a secret? Or just a small scratch?
I laughed at the breeze, tried to make it my friend,
But it blew me away, like a joke at the end.

Every gust gives a hint, it laughs as it goes,
'Follow me onward!', as if it really knows.
While I float with the leaves, I fumble and trip,
But it's hard to be graceful when you're losing your grip!

## The Uncharted Voyage

I set out on waters, with a boat made of dreams,
No map or direction, or so it seems.
The waves start to chuckle, the fish join the fun,
As I try to steer straight, but it's all just a run.

A whale gives a wave, says 'You'll never align!'
I grin back and respond, 'That's just by design!'
So I float with a giggle, through splashes and glee,
After all, the true journey is just being free!

# Charting a Course through Shadowed Waters

I set sail with a banana for a map,
Thought it would help, but I took a nap.
Woke up to seagulls laughing in glee,
Turns out they're the true captains, not me.

I steered by the stars, or what I thought were them,
But it was just a streetlight, shining so dim.
The fish seemed to giggle, the tides said, 'Oh, dear!'
I'm out here fishing for truth, not a dinner smear.

With winds that blew dreams into cotton candy,
I thought I'd go south, but got something dandy.
A world full of laughs, where every wave sings,
Turns out the treasure is just silly things.

So here I float in this crazy parade,
With a smile as my sail, and a joke as a trade.
The seas may get wobbly, the skies filled with gray,
But a chuckle can turn all your worries away.

# Embracing the Winds of Change

I tried to catch winds in a funnel cake,
But every sweet whiff just made my legs shake.
The breeze whispered jokes and tickled my ear,
As I danced with the gusts, sans a single fear.

I traded my map for a song in the air,
Found out my GPS was just a pet bear.
He led me through fields of jellybean bliss,
Where uncertainty wrapped me in a colorful kiss.

Each gust brought a giggle, an unexpected bend,
Who knew wild weather could be such a friend?
So I twirled through the chaos, wearing mismatched shoes,
While the clouds sang a chorus of 'You can't lose!'

I'm sailing on breezes that tickle my toes,
With a wink to the storms and a laugh at my woes.
Embracing each moment, oh what a delight,
With change as my partner, we'll dance through the night.

## A Journey Without a Guide

With no map in hand, just a grin on my face,
I stumbled quite gently through this wild space.
The roads twisted oddly, like spaghetti at lunch,
But each turn led me to a delightful crunch.

I asked a cow for directions, he said, 'Moo!'
Not quite the help that I'd thought would ensue.
Yet as I wandered with laughter around,
I found joy in the places I never had found.

The trees whispered secrets, the flowers would tease,
Their giggles and chuckles floated with ease.
I waved at a squirrel who danced on a line,
His cartwheels and flips were simply divine.

So here I am, lost in a world full of cheer,
With no map or compass, but the laughter is clear.
Each step is an adventure, each path is a rhyme,
In this whimsical world, I'm right on time.

## The Compass of the Heart

I searched for a compass, but found my own cheer,
With jellybeans guiding my way, oh dear!
They pointed me south to a land made of fun,
Where logic took breaks and silliness won.

With giggles as beacons, I stumbled quite deft,
Through marshmallow meadows, my worries bereft.
Each heartbeat a rhythm, each laugh like a song,
In this whimsical journey, I knew I belonged.

I followed the streams made of chocolate and cream,
And danced with the daisies while chasing a dream.
For wandering's sweetness is found in the art,
Of letting the world guide you, straight from the heart.

So here's to the compass that lingers within,
It spins with delight as we twirl and we grin.
In a world full of wonder, let laughter be free,
It's a journey best taken with joy as the key.

## Finding Meaning in Disarray

I lost my way at a crowded fair,
With cotton candy in my hair.
I asked a clown, he just laughed loud,
Said, "In the chaos, you'll find a crowd!"

My GPS is broken, it sends me wild,
To places where I've never smiled.
I asked a dog, he just wagged his tail,
"Just follow the scent, you'll never fail!"

I found a map that was upside down,
Said I should head towards a nearby town.
But "town" was just a giant shoe,
Guess the compass is broken, too!

Through tangled paths and funny signs,
Life's a circus with all its lines.
With laughter loud and joy on cue,
I'll skip on paths that lead to you!

## Serendipity's Compass

I woke up late, missed my ride,
Thought, "What a way to bide my stride!"
Took a left where I should've gone right,
Found a taco truck, what a delight!

With every twist, the adventure grows,
From carrots to shoes and garden gnomes.
The map said right, but I turned around,
Now I'm lost in the best taco town!

Met a squirrel who showed me the way,
With a nutty grin and a playful sway.
I said, "Where's the road to my café?"
He pointed, laughed, then ran away!

In the mishaps, laughter does bloom,
A joyful heart chases away gloom.
Life without plans is a hilarious ride,
With serendipity always as my guide!

## A Tattered Map

Once I found a map, frayed and torn,
It led to treasures, or so I was sworn.
But every "X" just found a cat,
Who napped in the sun, then gave me a pat.

I followed lines that went round and round,
Each twist and turn made no sense found.
I slipped on a puddle, quite the big splash,
All for a legend of pirate's stash!

The compass spun like a top on the floor,
Sent me chasing wild geese, oh what a chore!
But if life's a puzzle, I'm missing a piece,
With maps made of laughter, I'll never cease!

So here's to the roads that don't seem to lead,
To quirky encounters, and friends in need.
A tattered map may confuse the climb,
But in every mishap, there's joy every time!

# The Journey's Unknown Terrain

With no map in hand, I roam the street,
Every bump is a party, every crack a feat.
An unexpected twist to my daily grind,
Dancing with strangers, oh how kind!

I tripped over laughter, fell into cheer,
Spilt soda on shoes, but who needs fear?
Every misstep becomes a new tale,
With paths that twist like a winding snail.

A signpost says "Danger," but I just grin,
Life's rough edges are where I begin.
Who knew the wild could bring such delight?
Uncharted roads shine so bright!

So here's my toast to the lost and found,
To every wrong turn that spins around.
In the unknown, the fun just won't wane,
In this wild journey, it's joy I gain!

## Curves of the Forgotten Trail

In a land where the GPS fails,
I took a ride down wobbly trails.
With a map that was drawn by a cat,
I ended up lost in a farmer's hat.

The sign said 'left'; I turned right,
Now I'm arguing with a crow in flight.
The path twisted round like a noodle,
I think I just passed a bewildered poodle.

Rabbits giggle, and squirrels point,
As I stumble upon a hidden joint.
A picnic set up, sans any reason,
Turns out it's a festive squirrel season.

So, I munch on crumbs, feeling quite wise,
As a raccoon offers a side of fries.
In this silly maze of feathery fun,
I think I've discovered my own little sun.

## Serendipity's Dance on the Open Road

Fueled by joy, I hit the street,
With a playlist of tunes and two left feet.
I took a turn where the llamas graze,
And found a festival in a daze.

With balloons in hand, me and my crew,
Tried to tango with a big kangaroo.
He hopped away, to my great surprise,
Leaving my dance moves to criticize.

A tire rolled by, I ran for cover,
Landed in a pie—oh brother!
Berry filling goo with a hint of spice,
Now the birds think I'm a nice dessert slice.

Through laughter and crumbs, we spun around,
Til I found a treasure buried in the ground.
A compass? Oh no, just an old shoe,
But it danced with glee—it belonged to a kangaroo!

## Maps Written in Starlight

One night I looked up, gave stars a wink,
Trusting their glow, I forgot to think.
Drawn by a comet, into the fray,
I tripped on a cloud and fell into play.

A constellation whispered, 'Go this way,'
But I ended up in a cabaret.
With cats in tuxedos singing a tune,
I danced with a moonbeam, oh how we swoon!

My guide was a moth, so bold and spry,
He led me to laughter under the sky.
Dodging the puddles of starlit delight,
I thought, 'This is better than searching for light!'

At dawn, I awoke with glittery dreams,
Chasing the sun, or so it seems.
A map drawn in starlight? Well, that's a twist,
Who knew getting lost could be so blissed?

## **Finding Eden Beyond the Horizon**

There's a rumor of paradise over the hill,
With smoothies and sunshine, oh what a thrill!
So off I went, with flip-flops and cheer,
Ignoring the signs that just disappeared.

I've got a knack for mischief, you see,
Ended up in a place swarming with bees.
Dancing around, I dared not retreat,
For this honey was turning out rather sweet.

A goat with a monocle offered me tea,
'Eden's this way!' he bleated with glee.
I followed him straight to a disco ball,
Where critters were jiving, having a ball.

When the sun began setting, I thought, 'What a view!'
Eden's not perfect, but laughter rings true.
So here I remain, with wide-open eyes,
Finding bliss in the chaos, where fun never lies.

## Whispers of Intuition

In a world that spins and twirls,
My feet fumble, hair in curls.
With every turn, a giggle grows,
Trusting the vibes that nobody knows.

I waved to clouds, they waved right back,
As I stumbled down an old dirt track.
The trees gave wink, the sun gave cheer,
Who needs a guide when the sky's so near?

## The Road Less Remembered

On a path where I lost my way,
I tripped on roots, oh what a day!
Each step a comedy, a show of glee,
Hiccups of fate twirling round me.

The signposts giggled, they'd never been,
Where was I going? Oh, I don't keen.
With maps upside down, the sun in my eyes,
I just follow where the squirrel flies.

## Seeking Axes in a Spinning World

Around I spin, a dizzy chap,
Trying to find where I took a nap.
Axes and angles, all jumbled and wrong,
Yet the laughs keep me humming a tune so strong.

A pirouette here, a twist of the shoe,
In this circus of life, I'm the main show too.
Step right up, see the great feet flail,
Finding my way through a wobbly trail.

## The Art of Getting Lost

In the gallery where confusion reigns,
I'm painting pictures with wobbly gains.
Each wrong turn is a brush of gold,
Masterpieces made from stories untold.

With every stumble, I create a new dance,
Embracing the chaos, oh what a chance!
Life's a canvas, messy and vast,
And getting lost is my favorite pastime at last!

## Finding Home In Discomfort

In flip-flops on a snowy morn,
I tripped on my own zest for fun.
Lost my way in a shopping mall,
Found a donut shop instead, oh what a run!

My GPS is broken, who needs a guide?
I follow squirrels and their gossiping pride.
With every wrong turn, laughter grows bright,
At least I've got snacks for the long night!

Now I dance in the rain with my favorite hat,
Chasing my tail like a befuddled cat.
A map would be nice, but hey, who's to say?
Life's a circus, and I'm in the fray!

So here's to the mishaps and quirky trails,
To finding home where adventure prevails.
In every misstep, a lesson unfolds,
With a sprinkle of humor, the story is gold!

## **Sundown on the Road Less Traveled**

There's a sunset flashing on my left shoe,
Turned the wrong way but I'm still brand new.
Hitching rides with clouds as they float on by,
Who said I needed a map to fly?

My car runs on laughter and silly dreams,
Running in circles, or so it seems.
Every bump's a jiggle, every turn a twist,
Mistakes just add flavor, nothing is missed!

A raccoon sings karaoke, it's quite a show,
I join in boldly, stealing the glow.
Underneath the stars, we dance and sway,
With no strategy, we laugh anyway!

As daylight dims, and I munch my fries,
I smell adventure baked beneath the skies.
Who needs a guide when you've got a goofy grin?
With friendships like this, where do I begin?

## Paths of the Wayward Star

Stumbled on the wrong street and watched my shoe fly,
The stars laughed out loud, oh how they did try!
I pointed left and then I pointed right,
Wound up at a taco stand, a tasty delight!

Each fork in the road is a reason to cheer,
The detours are funny, so let's grab a beer.
With mismatched socks as my trusty allies,
I waltz with the daisies, beneath cloudy skies.

A hedgehog rolls by, playing hide-and-seek,
In the game of my life, I feel very chic.
With each silly stumble, I dance through the night,
For every wrong turn leads to pure delight!

So here's raising glasses to every surprise,
With laughter my compass, I'll rise and I'll rise.
On paths that are wobbly, a joyride we'll roam,
In this wild, whacky journey, I've finally found home!

## Unspoken Signs Along the Way

I read a sign that said 'This Way Home',
But it pointed to a llama, or maybe a gnome.
With a wink and a nod, I followed my nose,
Straight to a party where no one even knows!

Around every corner, a surprise awaits,
Like marshmallow clouds on picnic plates.
I misstep with style, like a dance on a vine,
Who knew lost could taste just like wine?

A penguin on skates said, 'Life is a dance!'
I'm twirling, I'm whirling, oh what a chance!
The rhythm of chaos, the beat of the bold,
In every miscalculation, new stories unfold.

So toss out the map, let's paint the air,
With colors of laughter, without a care.
Adventures await at each turn and bend,
With friends made of giggles, on this I depend!

## Echoes of Tomorrow

I set forth with my map all askew,
But the paths are just gnomes in a queue.
The trees seem to giggle, the rocks wear a grin,
Each step is a riddle, where to begin?

I asked a dog the way to the cafe,
He barked out directions, then ran off to play.
With every misstep, I dance like a fool,
Life's like a jigsaw, with pieces to drool.

My compass is broken; it spins with delight,
Pointing to breakfast in the heart of the night.
Chasing shadows and sipping the sun,
Who needs a direction when lost can be fun?

So here's to the laughter in paths unforeseen,
I'll follow each echo, though no one knows keen.
With giggles as guides and jokes up my sleeve,
Tomorrow's adventures are what I believe!

## Rusted Instruments of Guidance

I pulled out my compass, it squeaked like a chair,
It pointed to dessert, I stopped to declare.
My GPS laughs and throws up its hands,
In the land of the lost, pizza still stands!

With maps made of chocolate, I start to embark,
Each path is a treasure, a whimsical lark.
The stars are my friends, so I don't mind the mess,
In a dance with the moon, I'll surely impress.

I take a left turn, but somehow went right,
Got swept up by shadows, lost in the night.
Yet here in my folly, I stumble and glide,
With laughter as fuel, I drift like the tide.

So here's to the rust, to tools gone awry,
Embrace all the wrongs, let the good times fly.
For life is a circus, a pie in the sky,
So I'll juggle my joy, and forever say why!

## Between Dreams and Wanderlust

Between snores and giggles, I wake with a cheer,
My dreams took me places where logic won't steer.
I hopped on a cloud, now I'm spinning around,
The ground is a mystery that laughs without sound.

With sandals on feet, I leap into the day,
Chasing down wishes that whisk me away.
An old man with purple hair points to the sea,
"I'm looking for nothing! Come wander with me!"

The maps are just doodles, the roads are a game,
With every twist and turn, it's never the same.
In parks made of jelly, I sip on my dreams,
And dance with the clouds while the sun softly beams.

So let go of the reins; take flight on a whim,
The world's our playground, let's dive into whim.
With laughter as currency, we'll find where we roam,
Between dreams and wanderlust, I'm finally home!

## The Art of Getting Lost

I've mastered the art of going astray,
With a map that's made of confetti and clay.
I zig and I zag like a fish on dry land,
While my thoughts do the cha-cha, it's all so unplanned.

The coffee shop's closed, and the street signs all glare,
But a squirrel in a hat offers me a chair.
With acorns as snacks, we plot our great quest,
In this maze of confusion, I must say I'm blessed.

A detour to nowhere, a stop at the moon,
I sing to the stars, my favorite tune.
With a skip in my shuffle and joy in my heart,
Every turn is a canvas; I'm proud of my art.

So let me get lost, take a whirl and a twirl,
In the world of chaos, I'll joyfully swirl.
With giggles as my guide and daffodils near,
The art of getting lost is my grand souvenir!

## Trails of the Uncertainty

I took a wrong turn at the first big tree,
It led me to a place where ducks roam free.
I asked for directions from a passing crow,
He just cawed back, 'Man, I don't know!'

I followed a squirrel, thought he knew the path,
He darted up a tree, and I felt his wrath.
With branches scratching and leaves in my hair,
I laughed at my journey, well, isn't life fair?

A turtle passed by, moving slow yet wise,
I swear he winked at me with his small, beady eyes.
I took a seat thinking, 'This could be great,'
But he pulled out a snack, and I was too late!

So here I am lost but I don't really mind,
Embracing the chaos, I'm not hard to find.
With giggles and chuckles, let nonsense ensue,
In this silly adventure, I'm still me, still true.

## Wanders Without an Anchor

I set sail on a boat made of noodles and cream,
Thought I was clever, it was a wild dream.
I tossed out the map, it was just too boring,
Ended up at a bakery, and oh, I was soaring!

The baker, he laughed, said, 'That's quite a craft!'
'But you do know, pasta's not how boats are raft?'
I shrugged with a grin, grabbed a pie on the way,
You can't win 'em all, but you can eat today!

I met a lost penguin, with hiccups and flair,
He said, 'I'm off to find fish, do you care?'
I thought, 'Why not? Let's chase a good snack,'
And we waddled together with no looking back.

We twirled through the streets, making quite a scene,
Who needs a direction when you've got ice cream?
So if you see me wandering without any guide,
Know I'm just here enjoying this wild, tasty ride.

## The Labyrinth of Choices

I stood at the crossroads, what a bizarre sight,
One way leads to tacos, the other to fright!
Decisions, decisions, what's a girl to do?
I chose the tacos — yes, this feels true!

A man in a hat said, 'Careful, my friend,
That path to the left leads to a strange end.'
I laughed, took a bite, said 'at least it's a trip,'
While pondering if chips should be included with dip.

A chicken joined in, all feathers and sass,
'You should have seen me just walkin' past!'
I offered her salsa, she fluffed up with pride,
Together we danced down this taco-filled ride.

I stumbled on choices like socks in a drawer,
The more I pulled out, the messier the floor!
Yet here I remain, without much ado,
In this crazy maze of flavors and goo.

## Rhythms of a Roaming Mind

My thoughts were like butterflies, fluttering free,
I chased them through gardens, oh look — a bee!
But when I reached out to catch one in flight,
It buzzed past my nose, what a silly sight!

I tried to jot down each whimsical thought,
But my pencil went rogue, a true battle fought.
It danced off the page, leaped onto my nose,
I laughed at this chaos only life knows.

A lizard nearby gave a nod of approval,
Said, 'Join me in daydreams, they're simply grooval!'
So off we went roaming in our silly minds,
For who needs a plan when fun is what binds?

With each new distraction, I giggle and grin,
Just follow the rhythm, let the adventure begin.
For life's little winks — they're the best of the finds,
In this jumbled parade of our roaming minds.

## **Stones of Uncertainty**

I trip on thoughts, they're piled too high,
Each misstep sends me laughing, oh my!
Do I go left or perhaps right then?
Life's a puzzle without a pen.

My shoes are squeaky, they judge my fate,
They whisper secrets, oh, isn't life great?
I dodge the rain with a dance and twirl,
Who needs a map when you can swirl?

My phone's lost, but oh, what a thrill,
No GPS, yet I'm climbing the hill.
Each pebble's a story, a chuckle or two,
I'll figure it out, just like you do!

With every misstep, I grin ear to ear,
What's wrong with a squint, or a little more cheer?
So here I wander, so wild and free,
Life's little stones are the best part of me.

## **Stars That Refuse to Shine**

The night's all messy, like my hairdo,
Stars were invited, but I guess they're booed.
I squint and stare at the blank, dark pie,
Is that a star? Nah, just a fly!

Maybe I'm dreamin', maybe I jest,
The sky's on a diet, a limited fest.
I could wish on clouds, but it seems quite odd,
How do they sparkle? Just nod, give a nod!

I'll throw some confetti, with a wink and a grin,
If stars don't appear, let the silliness begin!
With giggles and chuckles, I dance on my toes,
Who needs bright lights when your spirit just glows?

So here's to the stars and their fancy retreat,
They missed the fun party; what a big feat!
As they twinkle away, I'll keep up the cheer,
For every lost star, there's laughter right here!

## Veils of the Unknown

What's behind that curtain? A ghost with a grin?
　Or maybe just my socks that I never pinned?
　I peek through the folds, the mystery's thick,
　Could be magic or a trick made with a click.

　Veils all around, they swirl and they play,
　　Where's the exit? Oh, lost again today!
　I tumble through shadows; I trip on my shoe,
　When life hides the answers, you just go 'boo!'

Behind every question, there's laughter, you see,
　I might lose my way, but I stay wild and free.
　When a veil drops low, just take it in stride,
　Who knows what's waiting on the other side?

Let's toast to the veils and their sneaky surprise,
　For every tap dance, there's wisdom that flies.
　In the fog of confusion, let's dance and sway,
　With each hidden answer, we'll frolic and play!

## Across Untrodden Ground

What's lurking ahead? A bear or a frog?
No path laid out, just a map made of fog.
Each step is a tumble, a giggle, a dash,
I'll hop like a bunny or tumble with panache!

The grass whispers secrets, the trees share their tales,
Who said this was serious? Let's wear our pails!
I leap over puddles and slide down the slopes,
Lost in the fun, I'm a bundle of hopes!

With every new twist, I find room for a grin,
What's life without mess? Just a dull violin.
The ground might be wild, but it's bursting with cheer,
It's not about roads; it's the fun we hold dear!

So here's to the paths that are winding and spry,
With laughter as fuel, watch my spirit fly high.
Across untrodden ground, with friends by my side,
Let's skip through the adventure, let joy be our guide!

## Myriad Threads of Fate

With strings that tangle, twist, and twine,
I step on toes, then sip my wine.
The paths I take, a circus show,
Clowning through life, and oh, the flow!

A GPS? No, that's too tame,
I'd rather roll the dice and play a game.
Each wrong turn sparks a laugh or two,
In moments silly, I find what's true.

Oh, where's my hat? It flew away,
Caught by a breeze, it joined the fray.
Chasing after fortune's tease,
In this chaotic dance, I feel at ease.

So here's to fate, that fickle friend,
May every mishap bring a bend.
With threads of joy in knots and fray,
I'll weave my laughter, come what may.

## **The Undrawn Map**

An undrawn map, my trusty guide,
Sailing through life, with eyes wide.
Each detour turns into a jest,
Together, always passing the test.

I thought I'd land on solid ground,
But prancing goats had me spellbound.
Taking selfies upside down,
Life's a fair game, wear that crown!

Lost my keys in the fridge again,
Found them stashed with leftover hen.
With every twist, a giggle found,
In folly's dance, I spin around.

Who needs a plan or sense of way?
I'll take the wrong turn, come what may.
In laughter's arms, I find my peace,
A cartographer's dream, a joyous lease.

# Fleeting Moments Amid Chaos

The clock ticks loud in raucous cheer,
While squirrels plot mischief, oh dear!
Chasing hearts and stray umbrellas,
In life's madcap race with whimsical fellas.

A dance with puddles, splashes wide,
I leap like a frog, no need to hide.
Each fleeting moment, pure delight,
In silliness, my spirit takes flight.

The coffee spills, a caffeinated art,
Fueling laughter from the very start.
Stumbling through the morning's haze,
Finding joy in clumsy ways.

So here's to chaos, life's sweet jest,
Embrace the mess and wear a fest.
In every moment, let laughter rise,
A fleeting spark beneath the skies.

# Finding Beauty in Errant Paths

On paths uncharted, I tend to roam,
With mismatched socks, I call it home.
Each stumble leads to a grand surprise,
A squirrel in glasses, oh how it flies!

I set my compass to 'whimsy' mode,
Wherever that leads, that's my abode.
A detour here, a turn to the right,
In the land of oddities, I find the light.

With muddy shoes and jokes to tell,
Each misadventure rings a bell.
In errant paths, I seek the fun,
Chasing sunsets, enjoying the run.

So here's my toast, to the lost and found,
In twists and turns, joy will abound.
With laughter as my only guide,
Life's a carnival, come take a ride!

## The Heart's Unsung Cartography

I set out for an adventure, brave and bold,
With snacks in my pack, and dreams to unfold.
But the map I used was something quite vague,
Leading me round like a lost little plague.

My friends all told me, "Don't take a wrong turn!"
Yet here I am, with much more to learn.
I followed a squirrel, it seemed to win,
But it led me to trouble, oh where to begin?

The compass just giggled, it spun round and round,
As I searched for a path that just couldn't be found.
Each step that I took felt like a game show,
Where losing is winning, and who really knows?

So here in the wild, with a backpack of glee,
I'll dance with the trees, let my spirit run free.
With no sense of direction, I'll choose to embrace,
The laughter in chaos, and life's funny race.

## Echoes of a Journey Unseen

I trekked through the forest, with coffee in hand,
Dreaming of places that weren't really planned.
A tree whispered secrets, I stopped to engage,
It told me my route was a joke on a page.

With GPS broken, and no clue in sight,
I stumbled on trails that gave quite a fright.
I followed a rabbit with a curious twitch,
And ended up stranded near a giant's old pitch.

The moon winked at me; how could I resist?
This journey was wild, how could I have missed?
Twisting and turning with laughter and cheer,
Becoming the map, no destination near.

So let's pause for a moment, and take a good look,
At the chaos that happens when we write our own book.
For in life's winding maze, there's fun to be gleaned,\nWith echoes of laughter in places we've dreamed.

## Lost Stars

They told me to follow, to look at the signs,
But I tripped on my shoelace crossing two crooked lines.
The stars were a mess, in a cosmic duet,
While my navigation skills were a hit or a miss.

I asked for directions from a wobbly chair,
It spun round and laughed, tossing soft cushions in air.
With each passing moment, I thought I might cry,
But then I just chuckled; who needs to know why?

Once a wise owl flew by, all serious and grand,
"Follow your heart, not the map in your hand,"
It winked as it soared, taking flight in the breeze,
And I just stood stunned, a mix of confusion and ease.

So now I'm adrift, in a starlit parade,
With twists and with turns, through the light and the shade.
In the galaxy's mischief, I've found the best part:
Each lost little moment is food for the heart.

## Wandering Without Maps

I'm on an expedition, or so I declare,
With a coffee-stained shirt and questionable flair.
No GPS needed, just whims to embrace,
I'll wander through life at my giggly pace.

I tripped over rocks, but who really cares?
Every bump is a story, a few funny glares.
My compass decided to take a short nap,
So I followed a duck, who forgot to wear a cap.

The clouds were my friends, they changed every hour,
Sometimes they looked like pizza, but never a flower.
I played hopscotch with shadows, leapt puddles with glee,
Every twist in the road was a riddle for me.

So here's to the journeys, unplanned and sublime,
To laughter and chaos, and a jig in the grime.
With shoes full of laughter, I'm ready to dance,
In this wacky adventure, I'll take any chance.

www.ingramcontent.com/pod-product-compliance
Lightning Source LLC
Chambersburg PA
CBHW051638160426
43209CB00004B/704